Martin Luther's
REFORMATION DAY
COLORING BOOK
Cari Haus

OCT 31

Copyright ©2021 by Waymark Books

Published by: Waymark Books

P. O. Box 7

Cedar Lake, Michigan 48812

Design: Olena Lykova

All rights reserved. No part of this publication may be reproduced, distributed, or transmitted in any form or by any means, including photocopying, recording, or other electronic or mechanical methods, without the prior written permission of the publisher, except in the case of brief quotations embodied in critical reviews and certain other noncommercial uses permitted by copyright law.

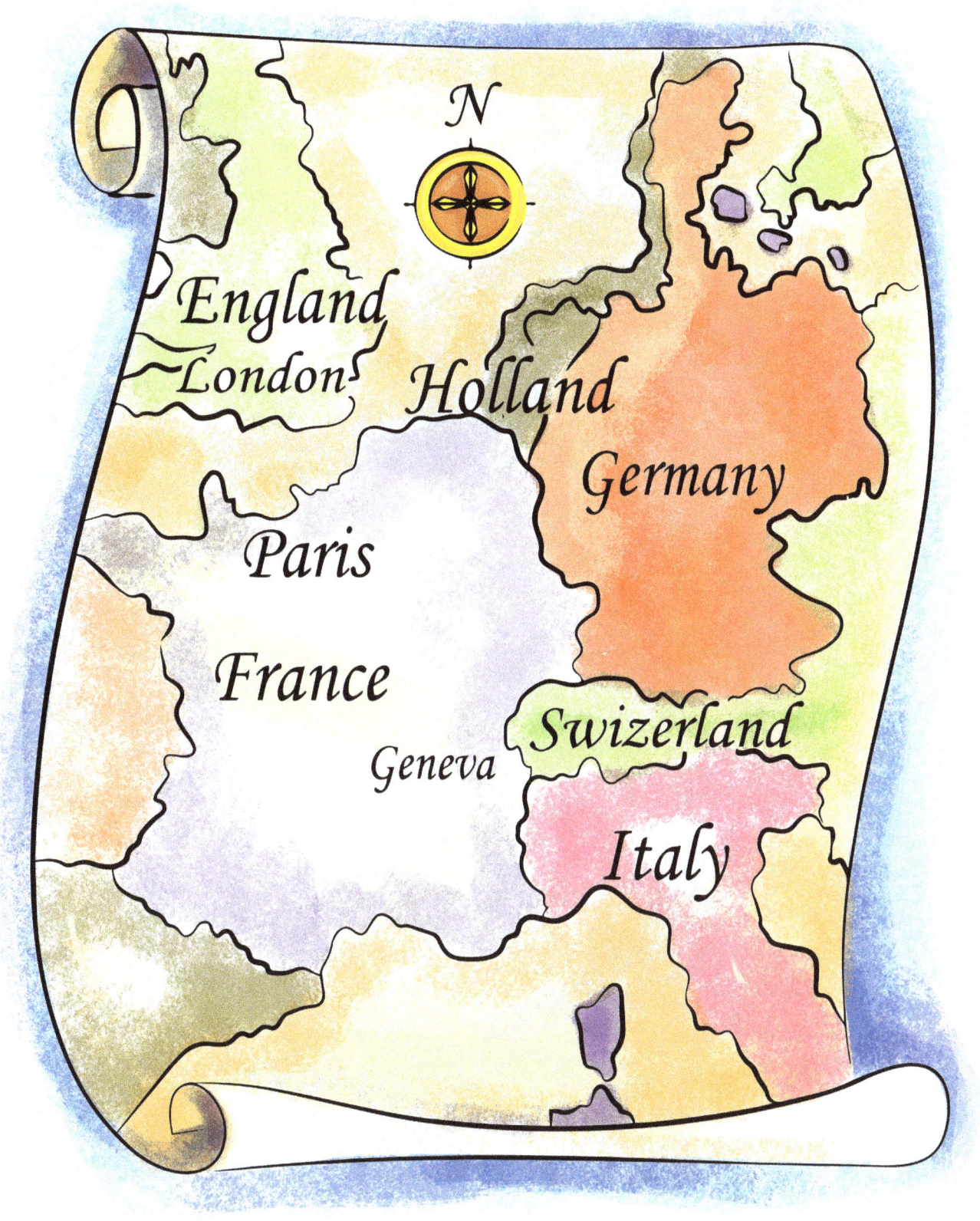

More than five hundred years ago, Martin Luther was born in the land of Germany.

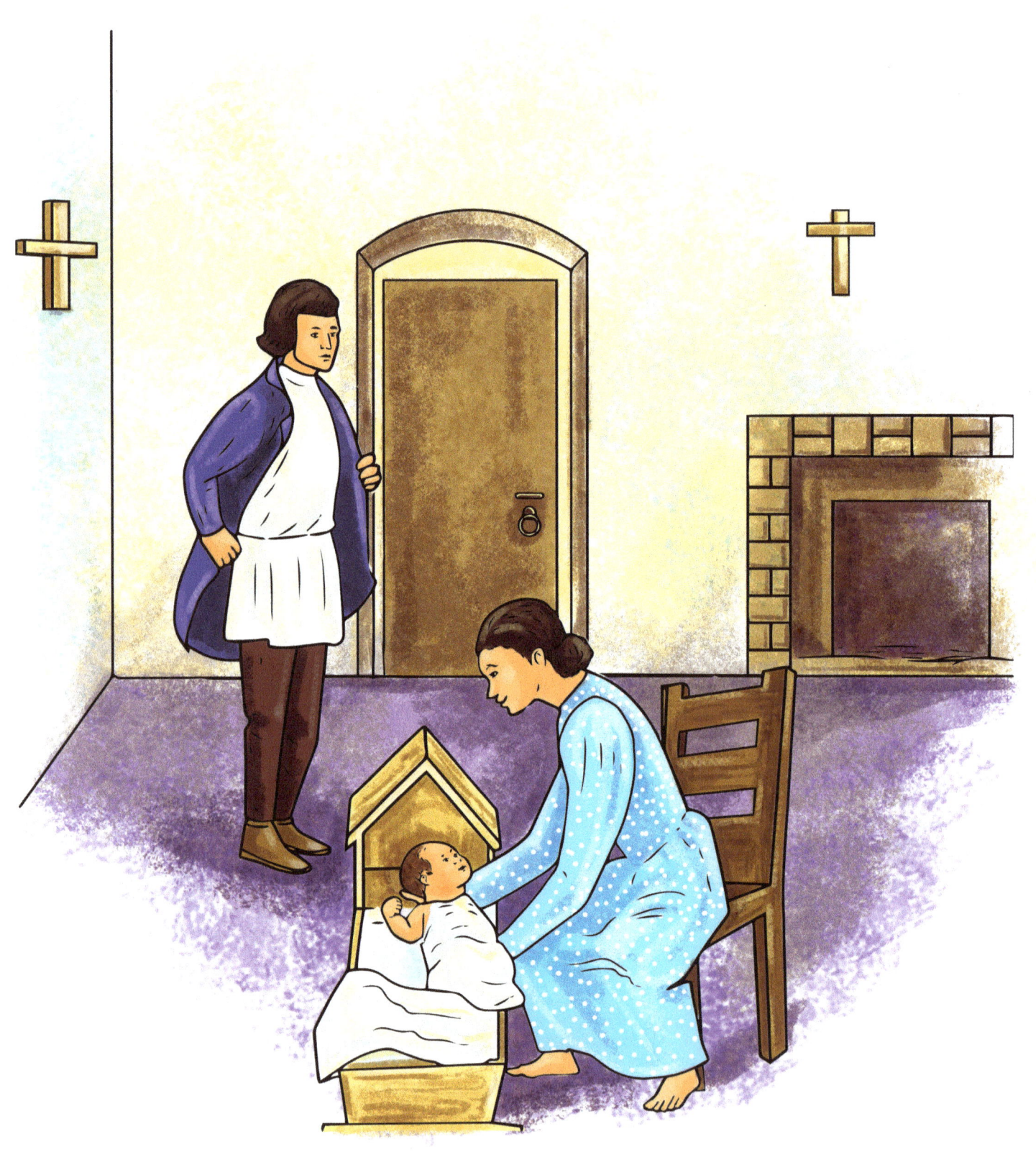

Martin Luther's parents loved Jesus. They wanted to raise their baby boy to love Jesus, too.

When Martin was a boy, his father had to do a lot of hard physical work. Martin's father wanted an easier life for his son, so he sent him to school. Martin studied hard. He was going to be a lawyer.

From a very young age, Martin Luther had a beautiful voice. This was a good thing, because Martin and other boys from his school often went out into the villages and sang for their supper. When they sang very nicely, the people gave them food to eat.

Then one day something happened that changed Martin's life. He was riding his horse when a lightning bolt struck nearby. "Help me Saint Anne!" Martin cried out. Martin promised that if God saved his life, he would become a monk. A monk was someone who spent his whole life trying to be close to God.

Martin Luther's father did not want his son to become a monk. But Martin felt like his promise was very important to keep. Martin went to live in a monastery, became a monk, and spent a lot of time trying to do good things. But sadly, Martin never felt like he really pleased God.

There was a Bible in the monastery, and Martin Luther started to read it. In the Bible, Martin learned that God doesn't ask us to try to be good on our own. We all sin, or do bad things, and this keeps us from God. But we can't clean up our hearts by ourselves. God has to do that for us.

At that time, a man named Tetzel was going around collecting money for the Church of Rome. "If you pay enough money to the church," Tetzel told the people, "God will let you into heaven." The Church of Rome didn't tell people the wonderful news of God's free gift.

Martin Luther read in God's word that you can't pay or work your way into heaven. By reading the Bible, Martin learned about God's wonderful plan. Martin learned that Jesus came to die on the cross, clean us from sin, and give us hearts that are pure and kind. And nobody had to pay for this gift!

HE HAS RISEN!

Martin Luther also read in his Bible that after Jesus died for our sins, He came back to life. That's what people mean when they say that He rose again. Jesus is alive! And He has already won the war against sin and death!

Martin was so excited about God's wonderful plan that he wanted to tell other people. He wanted others to know that God's gift is free! So he wrote something called the "95 Theses" that explained everything.

Your Word is a lamp to my feet and a light to my path.

T he word "theses" means a statement or theory—like something someone says that they believe can be proven. Martin Luther's "95 Theses" were taken straight from the Bible, the sure Word of God.

On October 31, 1517, Martin Luther nailed his "95 Theses" to the door of the Catholic Church in Wittenberg, Germany.

Other people liked and believed what Martin Luther wrote. They printed up copies and passed them around. Soon the "Good News" of Jesus and His free gift was sent all over Germany!

When Martin Luther began telling people that they needed to read the Bible for themselves, the leaders of the Church of Rome became very angry. "You will never get to heaven," they told Martin Luther. They said this because he wasn't teaching what they wanted him to. But Martin Luther kept on teaching and preaching, to the glory of God.

To keep Martin Luther safe, some of his friends hid him in the Castle of Wittenberg for a while. The castle was like a fort, a safe place where Martin could live and continue his work until it was safe to come out.

While he was hiding in the Castle of Wittenberg, Martin Luther had extra time to think and write. Martin knew that everyone should study God's Word. He knew that if people didn't read the Bible for themselves, they wouldn't have any way of knowing what really was right and wrong. Martin wanted everyone to be able to read the Bible.

So Martin Luther wrote out the words of the Bible in words that people could understand. Now they could read God's powerful Word—and learn about the wonderful plan of salvation—for themselves!

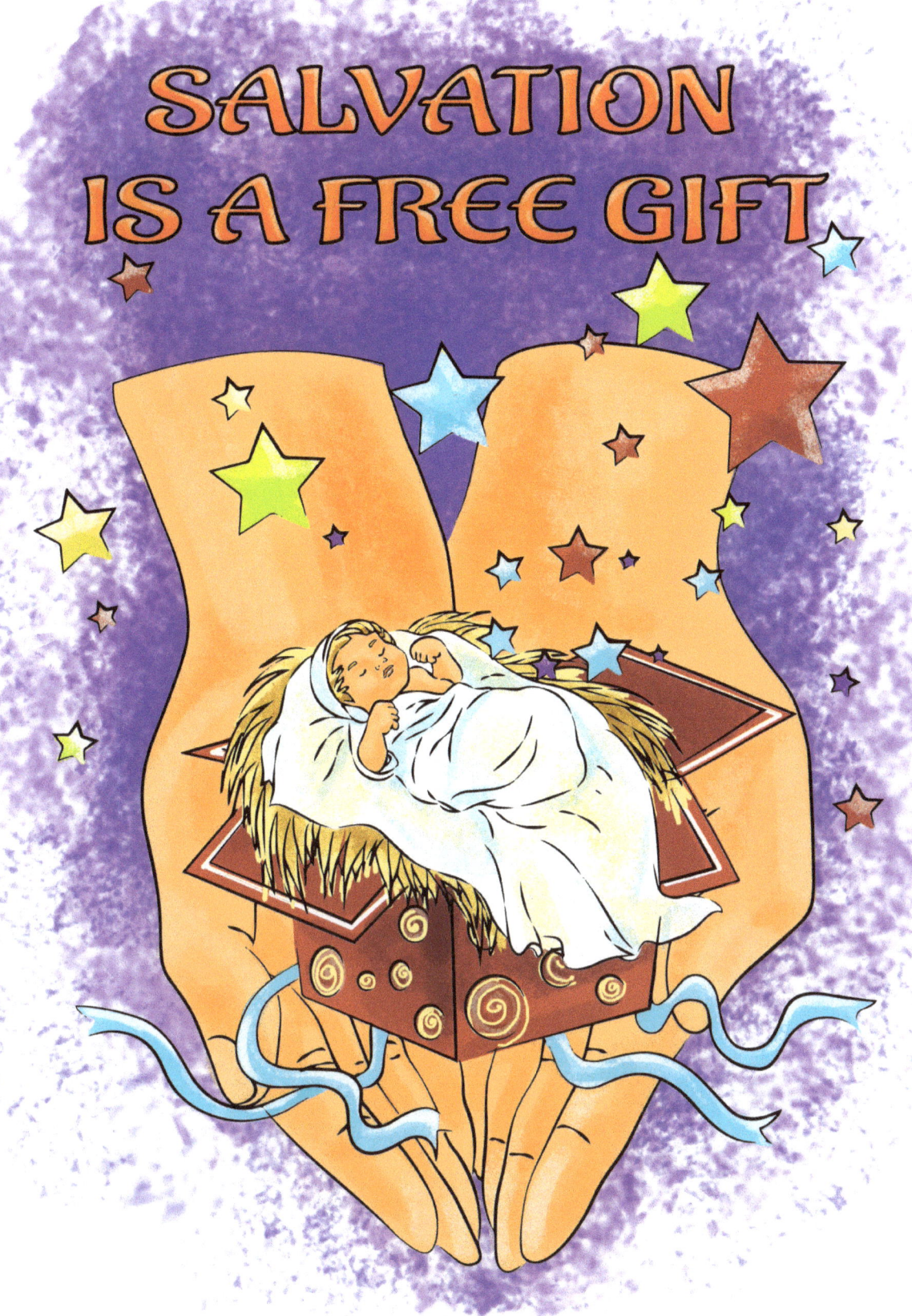

In the Bible, people could read for themselves that they should never have to pay for salvation. It is a free gift, from Jesus!

In the Bible, people could read the same things that Martin Luther had learned. They could read that "all Scripture is given by inspiration of God." (2 Timothy 3:16)

They could read the important Bible text that changed Martin Luther's life. That Bible verse, found in Romans 1:17, says "the just shall live by faith." To have faith is to believe in Jesus, and that's what we need to do!

A Mighty FORTRESS is our God,

a bulwork never failing.

Besides writing out the whole Bible, Martin Luther wrote a very famous hymn that is still sung today. That hymn talks about how strong God is and that God will take care of us. It says that God is like a safe place, a castle or a fortress. The name of that hymn is "A Mighty Fortress is Our God."

One day, Martin Luther left the Castle of Wittenberg and stood before the rulers and church leaders of the land. The rulers and church leaders asked Martin Luther to say that he had been wrong. They wanted Martin Luther to take back, or "recant," what he said. But Martin Luther knew that what he was teaching came straight from the sure Word of God.

I am **bound by the Scriptures** I have quoted and my conscience is captive to the **World of God**.

I cannot and will not retract anything.

I cannot do otherwise **here I stand,** may God help me, Amen.

- Martin Luther

Today, Martin Luther is famous for the words he said to the church leaders and rulers back then.

REFORMATION DAY

When Martin Luther nailed his "95 Theses" to the church door, he didn't know that many people would start reading the Bible for themselves and change their lives because of the good news about Jesus. But many people did change, or "reform." Martin Luther started what is know today as "The Great Reformation." To celebrate that important event that took place so long ago, many people now celebrate October 31 as "Reformation Day."

Although many years have come and gone since Martin Luther took his stand, there is much we can learn from his life. We can read the Bible for ourselves. We can stand up for the right. We can remember to live by the sure Word of God. We can also change for the good, thank Jesus for the free gift He has given and love Him with all of our hearts. With Jesus' help we can help start a "Great Reformation" both in our lives and in the lives of others—today!